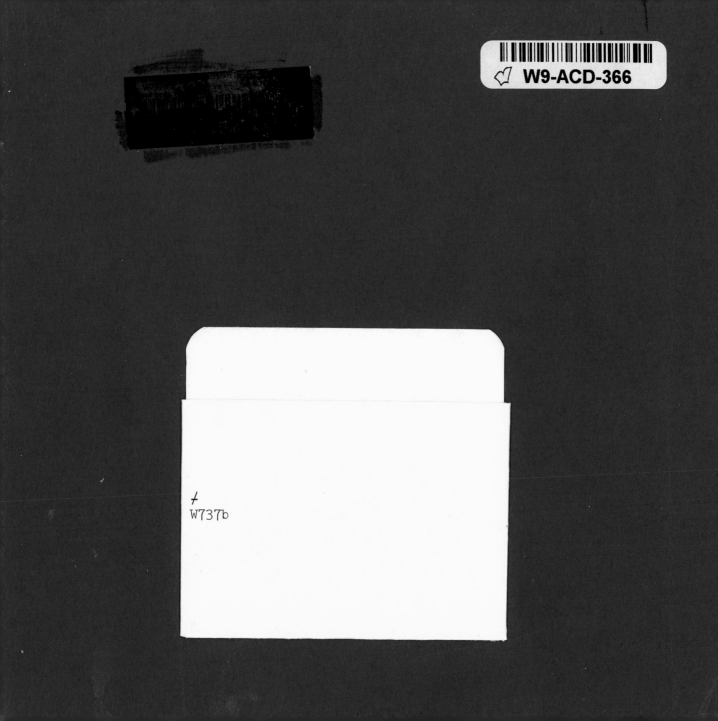

W737b

Bunk Beds

Harper & Row, Publishers
New York, Evanston, San Francisco, London

Bunk Beds

by
Elizabeth Winthrop
Pictures by
Ronald Himler

Library of Congress Catalog Card Number: 72-76499
Trade Standard Book Number: 06-026531-0
Harpercrest Standard Book Number: 06-026532-9

For Ian

in the top bunk

Bunk beds.
Willie on top,
Molly in the bottom,
closed in,
covered.

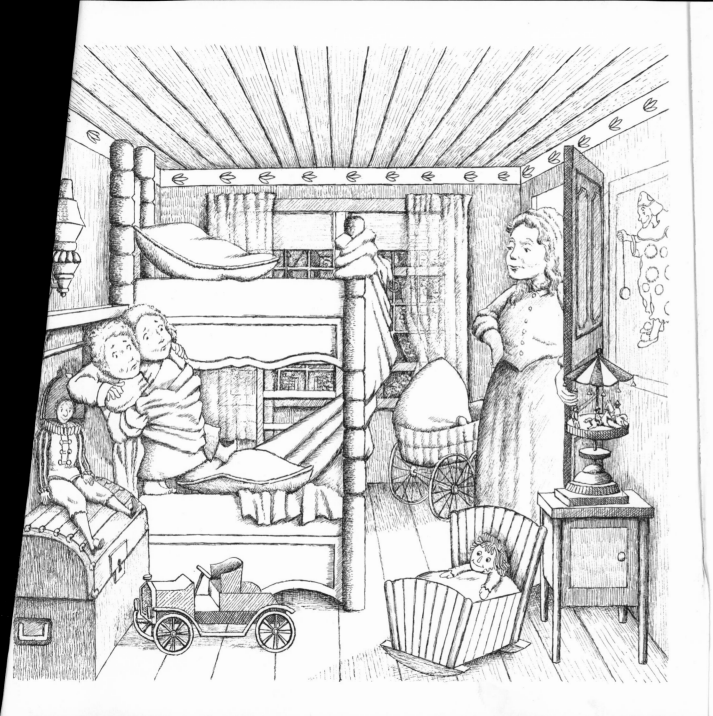

Molly pressed her feet against the mattress springs
and threw him up with a bounce.
"I am the captain of this ship,"
Willie whispered.
"You are the first mate.

"Hold on.
Bad weather ahead.
The ship is rocking.
The thunder is cracking and
the wind is trying to blow us away."
Molly threw her arms around the mast.
The waves rolled up over the deck.
"I can't hold on much longer,"
she shouted over the shriek of the wind.
"I'm coming,"
the captain cried.
"Hold on, mate."
The wind was whistling.
Lightning opened up the sky.

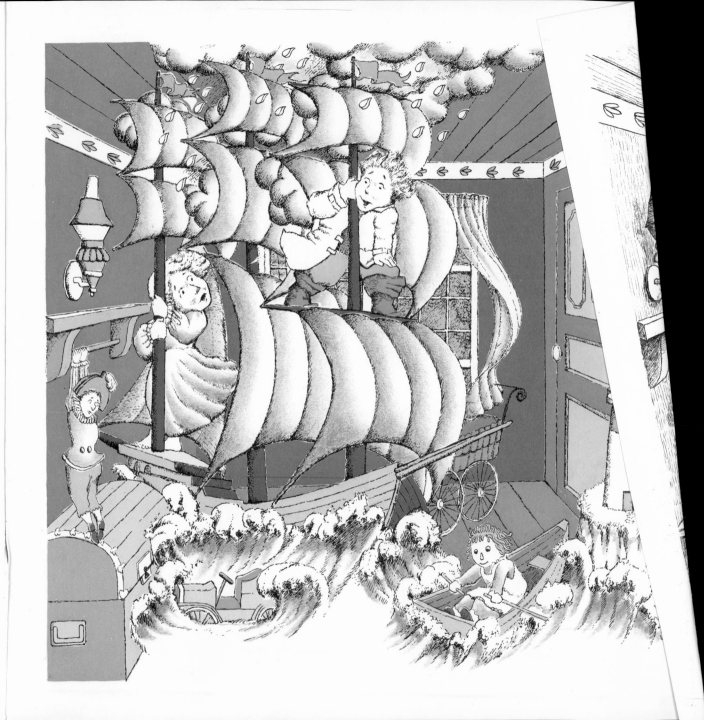

"What is all this racket?
Willie, what are you doing to your sister?"
"It's all right, Mum. I'm a sailor.
Willie was tying me to the mast."
"Well, come now, my brave sailors.
Back to your bunks.
The storm is over.
Time to go to sleep.
It's very late."

Thlunk.
The door closed.
The night light threw a small round glow on the far wall.
Outside, the cars mumbled by the window.
Their lights made shadow giants on the ceiling.
Willie dropped his sheet over the side.
"It's dark here in my house," Molly said,
and plumped up the pillows
on her living-room couch.
"I'm a burglar on the roof," Willie whispered.
"I'm sneaking in to get your jewels.
Lie down. Go to sleep."

Molly nestled into the pillow and
pulled the blanket up around her chin.
Her eyes looked closed, but they weren't really.
Molly could see a bare foot dangling,
looking for a place to climb down.
"I SEE YOU."
Rustle.
Squeak.
Whomp!
"Aaaaa-h-h."
"Don't murder me, please, sir.
I'll give you all the money you want.
All my jewels.
Oh help, somebody save me."

The burglar clamped a hot sticky hand
over her mouth.
"Hey come on, Willie. I can't breathe."
"Shh, stupid. Don't scream so loud.
I think I hear somebody."
Slipper footsteps.
Click…c—r—e—a—k…
Willie and Molly peeked around the sheet-wall.

Daddy looked very big, standing in the darkness
with the hall light shining behind him.
Slowly, Willie climbed back up to his bunk.
Daddy smiled a little.
The door squeaked shut behind him.

Nightness.

The window shade tapped against the pane of glass.

Outside, the street lights shone on green leaves.

Soft summer nightness.

A shout from down the street.

Willie's head dropped over the side.

His eyes looked at Molly, upside down.

"Those Carter kids are out again."

"It's not fair."

The church bell next door gonged.

Nine times.

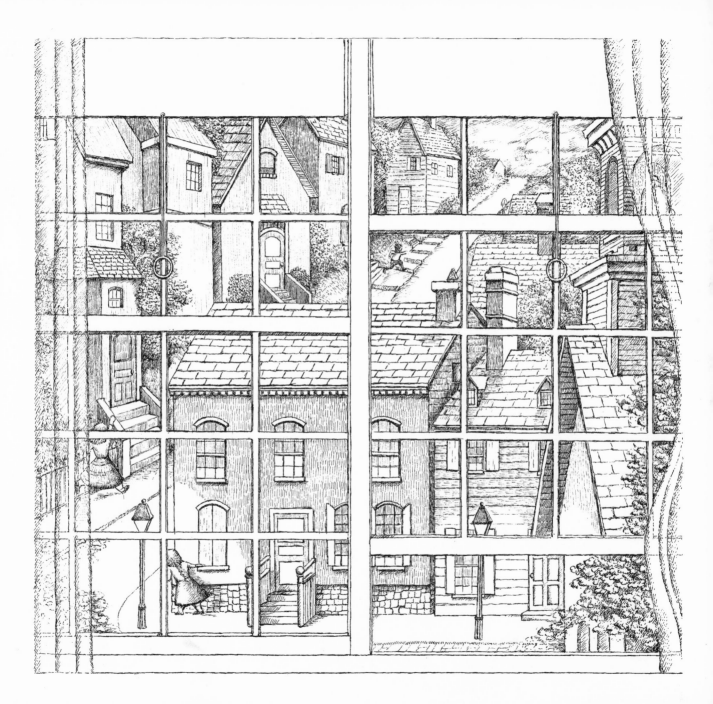

"Switch with me, Molly."

"Why?"

"I'm a car mechanic. I have to be under the car."

Molly crawled up the ladder and got into the car.

Willie climbed down the slats and

started clonking around with the engine.

"Make car sounds."

"Vroom. VROOM! Katapa, katapa, clunk."

"All right, lady, take your foot off the accelerator.
I'm going to put my hand in the engine now."

"Ssssh, Willie. Not so loud."

"Yep, just as I thought, it's the galloping piston rod."

"Oh dear. What's a galloping piston rod?"

"Well, it will cost you a lot of money,
and you'll have to leave it here a week."

Scruffle. Squeak. Whump.

"All right, rev her up again."

"Vroom! Vroom!"

"Louder."

"Hey, Willie, I don't wanna play anymore.
I just get to vroom."
"Okay."
"You wanna switch back?"
"Let's stay this way tonight, okay?"
"Well, just for tonight."

Flick-tick, flick-tick.

Clock sounds.

Outside, the green tree rustling.

Willie below.

Molly above. Night-listening.

From Willie's bed, Molly could see up over the rooftops.

Down in her bed, Willie was just a dark lump.

"Willie. Hey Willie?"

A sleeping dark lump.

Bunk beds.

Molly on top,

Willie in the bottom,

closed in,

covered.

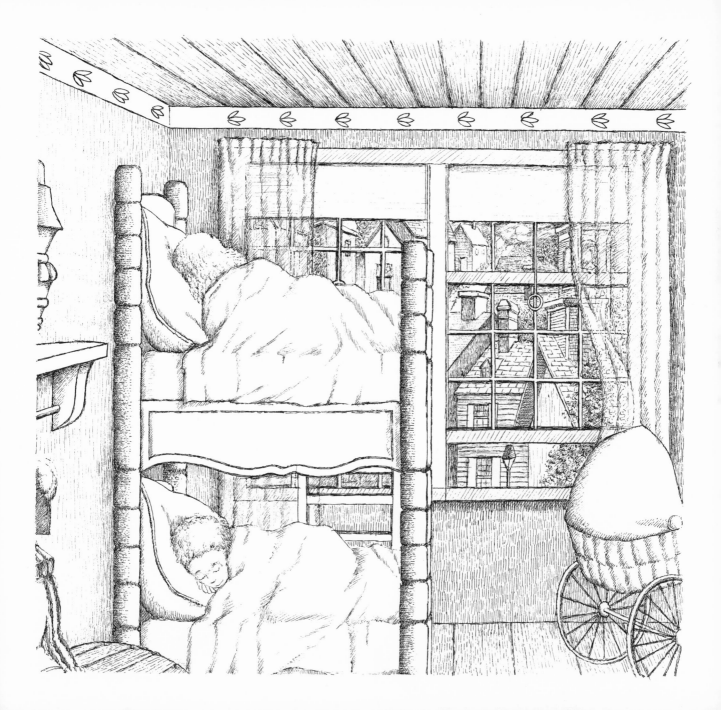